an illustrated story

The Lifeguard
Building Relationships
& Supporting Students

SHERRI NELSON
Illustrated by **ABBY JOHNSON-YOUNGQUIST**

The Lifeguard
© 2025 by Times 10 Publications
Highland Heights, OH 44143 USA
Website: 10publications.com

This story is a work of fiction inspired by a collection of educational experiences. Any resemblance to actual places, events, or persons, living or dead, is entirely coincidental. The advice and strategies contained in this book may or may not be suitable for your situation. You should consult with a professional, where appropriate.

All web links in this book are correct as of the publication date but may have become inactive or otherwise modified since that time. Name brands should not be considered endorsements by the author or Times 10 Publications.

Cover & interior design by Steven Plummer
Project management & editing by Regina Bell
Proofreading by Jennifer Jas

Paperback ISBN: 978-1-956512-71-7
Hardcover ISBN: 978-1-956512-72-4
eBook ISBN: 978-1-956512-73-1

Library of Congress Cataloging-in-Publication Data is available for this title.
First Printing: July 2025

For my family.

To my husband, Bjorn.
No one builds relationships better than you.

To my favorite educators, Rachel and Jennifer.
Keep bringing hope to the kids who need it the most.

Every child deserves a champion—an adult who will never give up on them, who understands the power of connection, and insists that they become the best that they can possibly be.

— RITA F. PIERSON, EDUCATOR

FOREWORD

I KNOW WHAT IT's like to be in over your head.

Years ago, I found myself caught in a cycle of poor decisions that led me to a dark and challenging place. But someone intervened at just the right time and shared a simple lesson that not only inspired me but also transformed my life.

I first met Sherri, the author of this book, when she invited me to speak to students in her school district about the power each of us has to positively influence our environment. A few years later, a speaking engagement brought me back to South Dakota, and we reconnected over coffee. That's when she handed me her manuscript for *The Lifeguard*.

I read it in one sitting on my short flight home. It struck me as a heartfelt, beautifully illustrated reminder of how much one caring adult can positively impact a student's life.

This book may be a quick read, but its message is powerful. Through the story of Ms. J and the community around her, we see that every student has the potential to succeed when compassionate adults build positive relationships, hold high expectations, and offer timely support.

What I love most is that this story reaches beyond the classroom. Being a lifeguard means helping students navigate the turbulent waters of school and life until they can swim on their own. It champions compassionate school personnel who choose to make a difference in the lives of our next generation. It also honors community volunteers from local businesses, healthcare, public safety, and many other roles, including retirees and college students who mentor students.

It only takes thirty minutes a week for you to make a meaningful difference, too.

It can be as simple as reading with a student, sharing lunch, playing catch, offering a listening ear, or being a trusted thought partner. These moments matter and make you part of this story.

Anyone willing to be a steady presence for a student trying to stay afloat has the power to make a difference. I've seen it time and again—ordinary people stepping in at just the right moment to make an extraordinary impact.

As you read, I hope you'll reflect on who might need a learning lifeguard in your school community. And more importantly—are you willing to be one?

This book is your invitation to dive in.

— DAMON WEST, BEST-SELLING COAUTHOR OF
THE COFFEE BEAN

HOW I BECAME A LIFEGUARD

IT WAS A scorching summer evening in northern Indiana. Danny, Jayson, and I had just finished dinner with the school administrators, who had invited us to share our strategies for helping all students experience success.

Before heading back to our accommodations, we decided to scope out the local landscape and discovered a lakeside beach filled with children playing in the sand and splashing in the water. As we walked toward them, the lifeguard made a brief announcement: "Attention, all swimmers! There will no longer be a lifeguard on duty. You are now swimming at your own risk. Thank you and good night."

I watched the lifeguard retrieve his rescue buoy, descend the tower steps, wade through the beachgoers, saunter to his car, and drive away. My worried eyes turned back to the children frolicking in the water. I swiftly scanned the shoreline. *What if something happens? Who's watching out for the inexperienced swimmers now?*

A similar situation unfolds in schools across the country. They all have students who, without sustained surveillance and reliable rescue techniques, may be in danger of academically drowning. Do educators say, "We tried," and walk away? Or do they practice prevention protocols and follow through with systematic responses to ensure all students experience academic success?

For the past thirty years, as a teacher, administrator, consultant, and parent, I've seen what happens when underperforming students are left unattended. Most struggle academically to keep their heads above water, and tragically, some are pulled under.

I didn't want that outcome for my children or anyone's children.

The future of our society relies on producing a well-educated workforce. Studies show that communities composed of educated individuals experience lower crime and greater prosperity. We can invest in our youth now ... or pay the price later. Hence, I've spent the last decade serving students and training school personnel and community volunteers to act as learning lifeguards.

I hope this simple story inspires you, your school personnel, and members of your community to vigilantly keep watch on your learners and wholeheartedly dive in when struggling students need assistance.

— SHERRI NELSON, AUTHOR OF *THE LIFEGUARD*
AND *LEARNING LIFEGUARDS*

The Lifeguard
Building Relationships
& Supporting Students

Lifeguards support swimmers.

Learning lifeguards support students.

It was almost five o'clock. Mya's summer
vacation would begin in two days ...
but only if she finished her research paper.

With the excitement of the impending summer, you'd expect to find Mya at the kitchen table in her home, intently writing while a family member prepared dinner and supervised her work session.

Perhaps this was the scenario for many students that day, but not for Mya. No one was home, and there was no kitchen table.

Mya's academic goals and support came from me.

I was Mya's learning lifeguard.

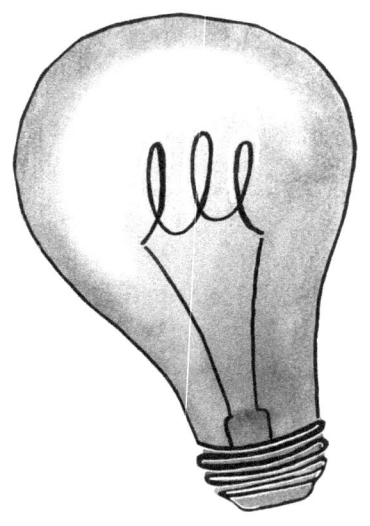

Mya was a bright girl.

In fact, she had developed an extensive vocabulary from her love of reading.

Mya often stayed up late finishing novels she had started earlier in the day, even as her list of incomplete class assignments grew longer and longer.

Her research paper was two weeks overdue. With persistent prodding from her language arts teacher, Mya had developed an outline, thoroughly researched her topic, and taken several pages of notes over three weeks. Despite that solid start, she hadn't used her time wisely and never finished the essay.

A few years before, her teacher would have simply sighed and entered a zero in the grade book, but not anymore.

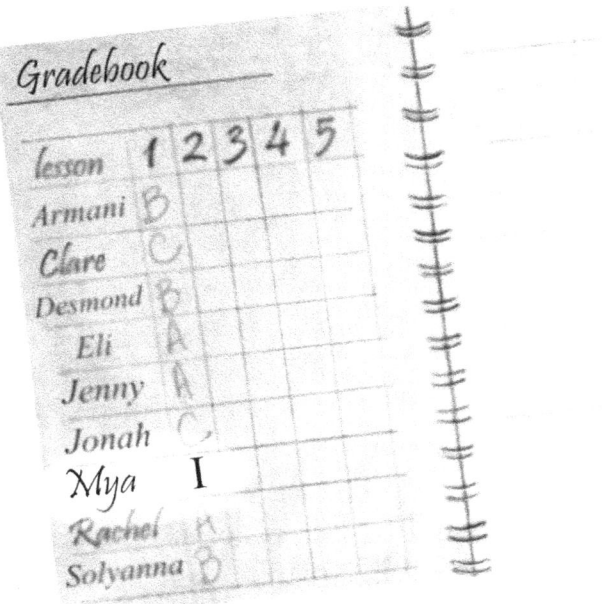

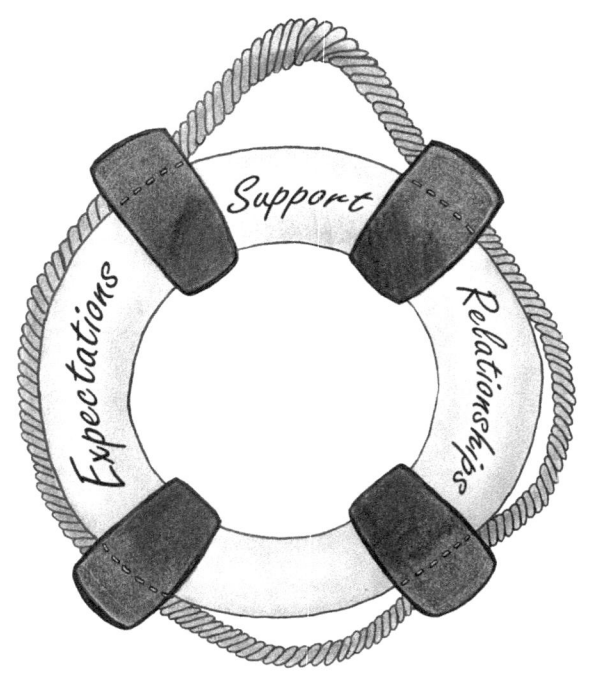

Now, we had a team of volunteer learning lifeguards in place at our school.

Like many other educators, we learned that all students can achieve high levels of learning if adults cultivate caring relationships, collectively hold all learners to high expectations, and provide academic support to struggling students.

However, the responsibility of helping all students reach their full potential couldn't rest solely on the shoulders of a few; it would require a committed team of school staff and community volunteers working together.

Research shows that just one trusted adult can have a profoundly positively influence on a child's life. We imagined the life-changing impact we could make in our school and community if every staff member fostered an academically supportive relationship with at least one struggling student.

In our school, every adult became a learning lifeguard.

Educational assistants helped students finish assignments before school.

Supervised high school and college students earned credits by tutoring other students during their open period. Teachers clarified misconceptions and retaught critical content at the end of their school day.

A custodian mentored a disruptive boy, more familiar with the principal's office than any classroom, by inviting him to tinker with tools and help with repairs around the school.

The librarian offered her desk as a quiet place for a distracted student to complete her homework.

The school secretary helped an unorganized student determine which assignment to tackle next.

The basketball coach checked in daily to ensure the struggling sibling of a varsity athlete made it to school.

Community members volunteered thirty minutes of their time each week to mentor the students who needed supportive relationships the most.

Anyone who had the heart to help our students and was committed to the journey was a learning lifeguard.

The purpose of the lifeguard was not to replace parents, caregivers, or classroom teachers. It was to provide additional support for students like Mya and empower them in their learning.

Effective Learning Lifeguards:

- ✓ Love kids, and the kids know it.
- ✓ Project positivity, yet are firm when necessary.
- ✓ Are team-oriented.
- ✓ Work adeptly with students and staff.
- ✓ Maintain high expectations for all learners, even those who don't yet have high aspirations for themselves.
- ✓ Boldly act with passion and purpose.
- ✓ Bring hope to students who need it.

We were investing in the future of our community by ensuring every student had an adult advocate and the best possible chance to succeed.

Now, several days before summer break, this resilient teenager sat cross-legged on the floor amid papers and sticky notes with a laptop perched on her knees. She was fully engaged and feeling supported in her learning journey.

I met Mya six weeks into her eighth-grade year. She was struggling with assignment deadlines, easily distracted, and chronically tardy to school. Teachers reported that she frequently missed the instruction critical for completing her assignments, and they didn't have time to get her caught up when she overslept.

Chapter Three
More To Her Story

When I asked Mya why she was always late to school, she shrugged and avoided my eyes. "I'm just tired," she mumbled.

A wise mentor once told me, "Every student has a story." I knew there had to be more to Mya's story.

Children begin learning from the moment they're born, and their home environment shapes their initial views about learning. The research is clear: Families who supervise, support, and maintain high aspirations for their children increase their chance of being successful students.

So, I attempted to contact Mya's parents to relay my concerns and launch an emergency rescue plan.

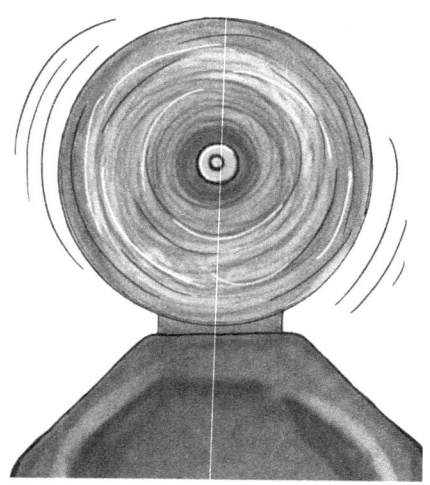

My first few attempts resulted in the echo of unanswered rings.

I persisted and kept calling.

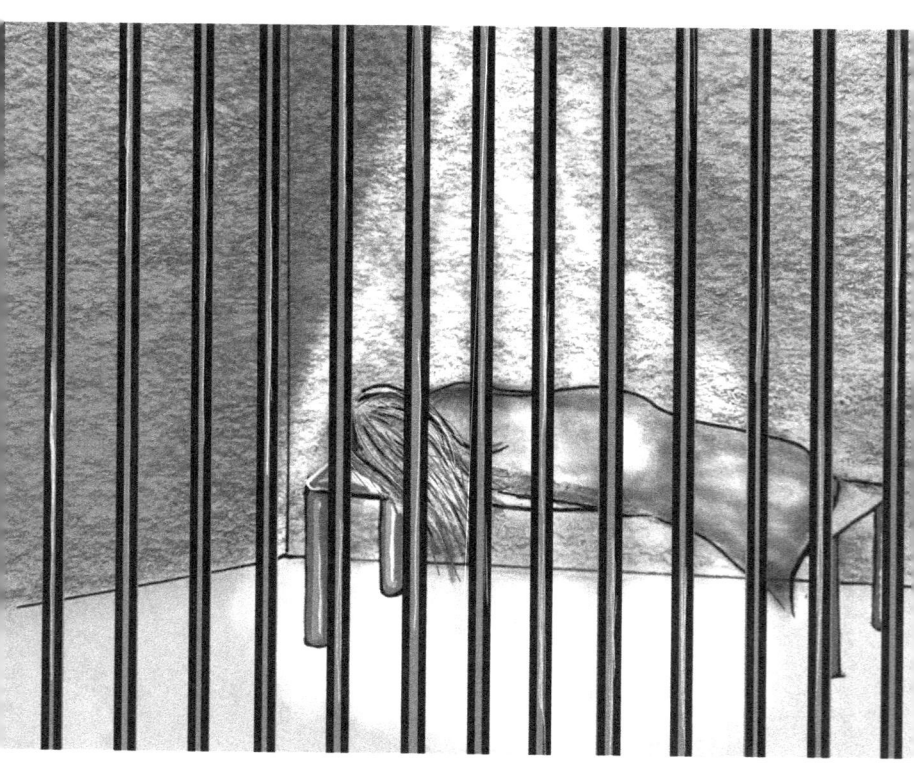

Eventually, Mya's grandmother answered
the phone. I asked to speak to Mya's mother.
"She's in prison," the grandmother snipped.
Why didn't we know this?

I introduced myself and explained the reason for my call. To my surprise, Mya's grandmother recognized my name, and her tone softened. I discovered that her daughter, Mya's mother, was a former student of ours who had muddled through her middle school years and eventually failed out of high school.

Back then, we didn't have lifeguards on duty. We operated with a "sink or swim" mentality.

When I met with Mya again, I mentioned that I had spoken with her grandmother. Her eyes widened, and then she whispered, "I didn't want anyone to know ... about my mom." I assured her that she could trust me with this information.

Sadly, living in the same community for more than twenty years, I'd seen generational families repeat tragic mistakes. After speaking with her grandmother and gaining Mya's trust, I felt the weight of the challenges she faced and knew she would need extra assistance if she were to acquire the skills and knowledge she needed to be ready for a career or college.

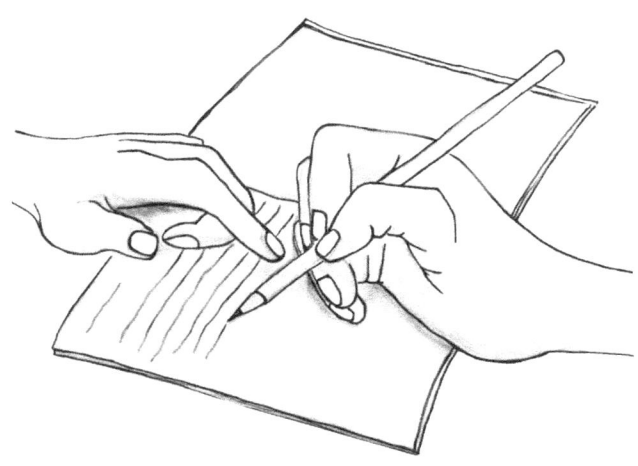

And, so, my rescue shift began. For the remainder of her eighth-grade year, I committed to being Mya's learning lifeguard.

I discovered early on that Mya had a special connection with her grandmother. "I don't know what I'd do without my grandma," Mya often said.

When parents and guardians are actively involved in their students' education, the students tend to perform better academically, demonstrate higher attendance rates, and are more likely to graduate. Knowing this, I cultivated a home-to-school relationship with Mya's grandmother by calling often to update her on her granddaughter's progress.

To strengthen their academic bond, I occasionally invited Mya's grandmother to school to sit with Mya and provide motivation and support as she worked on her assignments. Although it was challenging to find times that suited her grandmother's work schedule, it was worth it.

Mya's eyes lit up whenever her grandmother attended our study sessions. "I work harder when Grandma's watching," she confessed with a small smile.

My relationship with Mya hadn't formed
overnight. Like the erosion of sand along
the sea, our progress was often impeded by
setbacks.

I frequently found myself questioning Mya's actions and decisions.

She was often apathetic and uncooperative. Mya claimed she didn't need help, going so far as to say, "I can do my assignments. I choose not to." When her sass didn't deter my lifeguarding mission, she often pleaded, "Just let me fail!"

I had learned that, inevitably, when struggling students were held accountable for learning, they would say and do things to test our patience. I tried not to take Mya's defiance personally and reminded myself that she was a child who was still learning how to control her emotions.

And when I began to second-guess my lifeguarding abilities, I reached out to a few other lifeguards for strategies and support. "We've been getting along great, and now we've hit a wall. I don't know what else to try."

One teammate responded, "You just have to keep showing up."

Another lifeguard added, "And don't be afraid to change your approach if it's not working."

"I guess it's all about being patient and flexible," I said. We agreed that keeping every student afloat required patience, persistence, and agility.

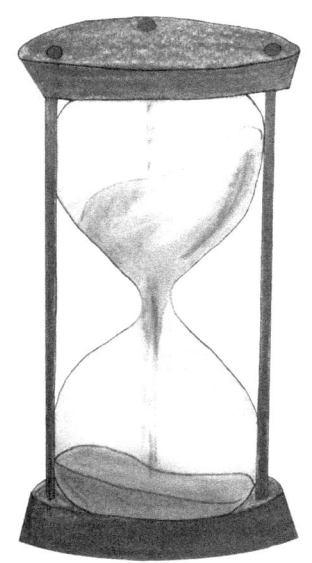

Developing trust took time.

Being present took time.

Building rapport took time.

There was no one-size-fits-all strategy. I followed Mya's lead and continually searched for new ways to connect with her.

My approach changed to accommodate the high and low tides of Mya's life, but I continued to provide support and hold her accountable for learning.

When we butted heads, I resisted the urge to have the last word.

No judgments. No lectures.

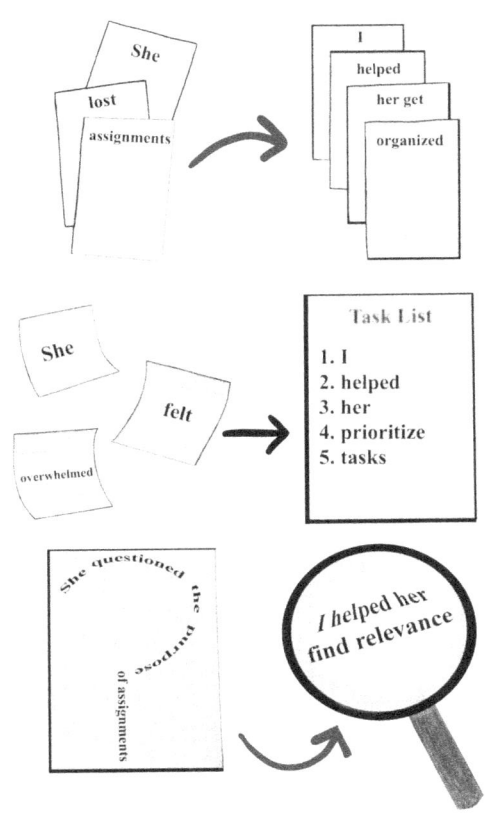

Instead, I chose to calm the chaos by helping Mya practice productive learning strategies and habits.

Slowly, Mya's resistance began to dissipate.
    But little did I know that behind the scenes,
a storm was brewing.

Mya had been attending school more regularly and seemed to look forward to our productive work sessions. When she didn't come to school one day and no one answered her home phone, I had a hunch something was wrong.

"I'm really worried about Mya," I said to the principal. "She's usually good about letting me know if she's not coming."

The principal nodded, a concerned look on his face. "Let's go check on her."

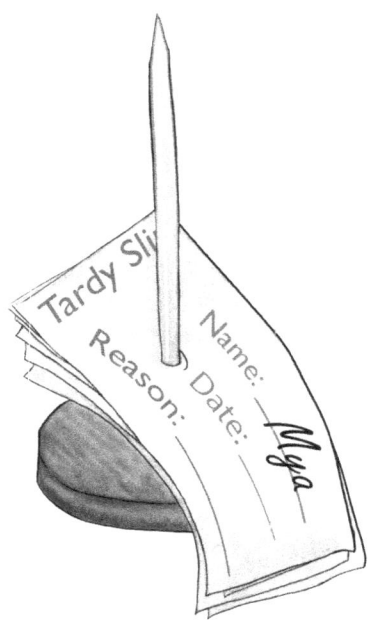

We drove to Mya's grandmother's home, a
squat, one-story house with peeling gray
paint. The neighbor's dogs barked from behind
their chain-link fence as we approached the
front door.

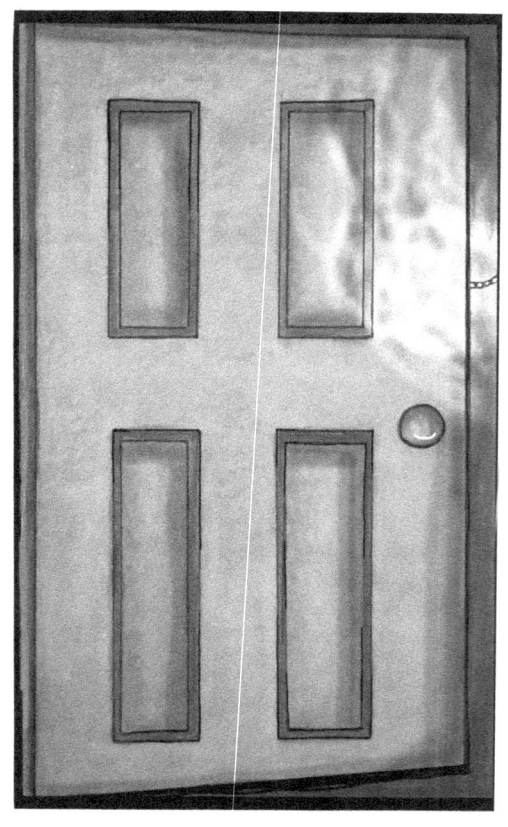

Our relentless knocking eventually paid off, and the door opened. We were greeted first by the smell of cigarette smoke and then by a person—but it was not Mya or her grandmother.

Her posture was a little hunched, and the lines around her mouth told a story of struggle, but when her eyes connected with mine, I recognized the former student who had once walked the halls of our school. Mya's mother, recently released from prison, had moved into the home.

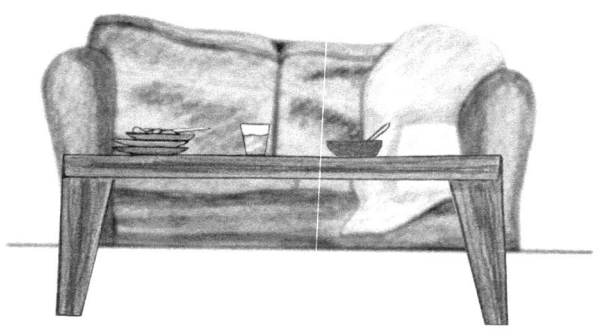

The curtains inside were all drawn, making the house look even smaller than it had from the street. I could see a pillow and blanket on the sagging sofa and wondered if the living room was also serving as a bedroom. The scratched coffee table was littered with dirty dishes, which made sense since I didn't see a dining table in the tiny kitchen that was located beyond the living room.

No wonder Mya had rolled her eyes when I asked if she had a study space to finish her schoolwork in her grandmother's home.

We brought Mya's mother up to speed on the situation, and her forehead creased with concern. "I dropped her off at school this morning," she said with a shaky voice.

Then she sighed and admitted, "But things haven't been going well at home lately."

She paused before continuing, "Mya's been pushing me away. I'm trying to reconnect, but she won't let me in. And my mom ... she's exhausted. Working two jobs and trying to keep the peace between the two of us is wearing her down."

The weight of her words explained a lot, but we still needed to find Mya.

Mya wasn't in the little house. She wasn't at school.

It was official—Mya was missing.

With an all-hands-on-deck approach, we spent the rest of the day trying to locate Mya. Our surveillance video showed her walking away from campus rather than entering the school in the morning. We spoke to her grandmother at work. We knocked on neighbors' doors. We questioned Mya's circle of friends.

No one knew where Mya was, but many agreed to help spread the word and to join the search.

Thankfully, the police finally found her late
that evening, walking alone on a side street.
She had spent the entire day hidden in a city
park restroom.

When Mya arrived at school the next morning, sadness surrounded her like a dark cloud. We sat in silence for several minutes before I revealed that I knew how she had spent the previous day.

"I'm so glad you're here, Mya."

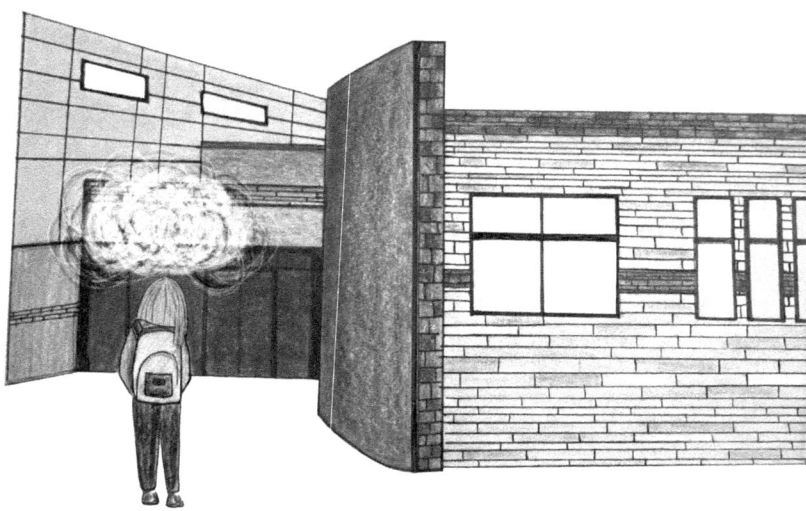

With her eyes veiled by tears, she murmured,
"I wish I were still there." It hurt my heart to
hear that Mya felt her situation had become
dire enough to choose any refuge in a storm,
anywhere she could be alone, even a restroom.

"Is there something you need me to do? Or
do you want me just to listen?" I asked.

"Just listen," she whispered.

As Mya's learning lifeguard, I knew every interaction with a young person was an opportunity to positively influence the next generation, even in some small way.

I could not erase her challenges, but I could help her develop the skills and confidence to face them. I would neither give up on her, nor would I allow her to give up on herself.

Just as heavy winds, crashing waves, and dangerous currents disrupt conditions at a beach, contentious interactions with friends, family, and school personnel affected Mya's attitude. They forced me to alter my approach continually.

I scheduled a home meeting with Mya's
mother and asked the school counselor to join
me. We attempted to reengage her with her
daughter's education. "Mya has been making
excellent progress toward her academic goals,"
I explained.

We encouraged her to resume her parental
role by maintaining the study routines that
were contributing to Mya's success.

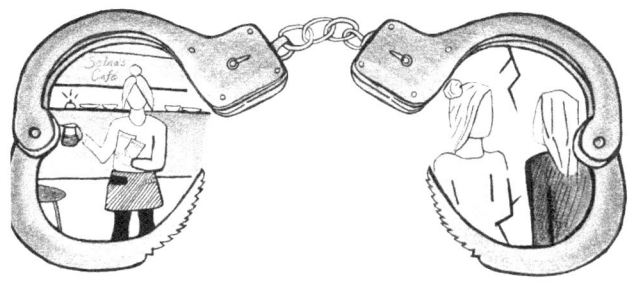

As our conversation continued, though, I sensed that while Mya's mother cared deeply for her daughter, adjusting to life after incarceration was crushing her. She tearfully divulged that her new job wasn't going well and her attempts to connect with Mya continued to be met with resistance and rebellion.

It became clear to me that it would be difficult for Mya's mother to provide academic support for Mya when she was struggling to keep her own head above water.

Instead, I assured her that we would do whatever it took to keep her daughter on track to obtaining her high school diploma.

"Thanks, Ms. J," she said quietly, looking at her slippers instead of my face. Her guarded expression was the same one I remembered from the days when she sat at the back of my classroom as a teenager herself.

"You know why I always liked you?" Mya's mother continued. "You never had favorites. It didn't matter how smart we were or who our parents were, you just wanted everyone to do their best, and you helped anyone who needed it."

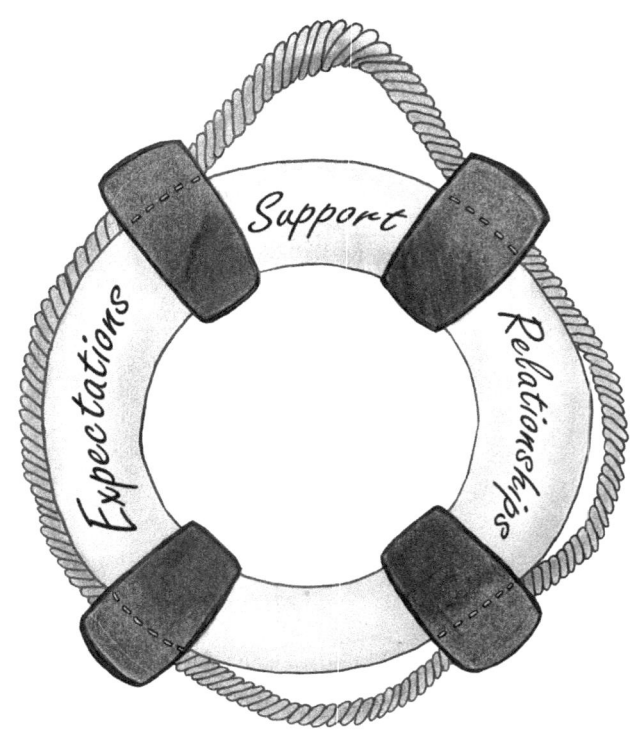

As I thanked her, it occurred to me that while parents and guardians were the most influential individuals in a child's education, any adult could be a close second if they consistently cultivated caring relationships, held young people to high expectations, and provided extra support to struggling students.

To turn the tide at school, we focused on what we could control between 8 a.m. and 4 p.m. We adjusted Mya's schedule so that she spent her lunch period and after-school time in my office, working on her assignments, while I attended to my to-do list nearby. I was there if she needed help, but mostly, I provided encouragement and a space where she could focus.

One day, she looked up and revealed, "I like working here. It's quieter than my house." That moment warmed my heart. It wasn't just about the calm space; it showed that her trust in me was continuing to grow and she felt safe and supported.

With six weeks of school remaining, Mya accepted my challenge to submit all her assignments before the final school assembly. We printed her long list of missing assignments and mapped out a plan to make her intention become a reality.

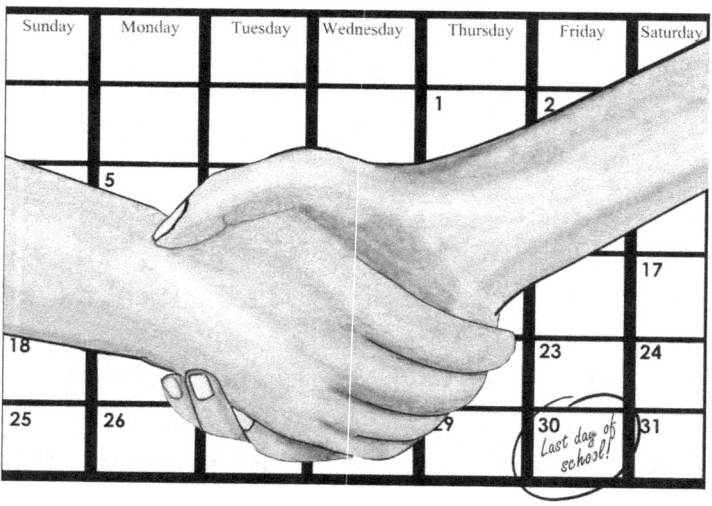

Missing Assignment List

- ☑ Easy Assignments
- ☑ Short Assignments
- ◯ Art Assignments
- ◯ Writing Assignments
- ◯ Math Assignments

To build momentum, we tackled the easiest assignments first, the ones that would take the least amount of time to complete. A look of pride filled Mya's face each time she physically crossed off an item on her list. As she gained confidence, we dove deeper and took on the more challenging tasks.

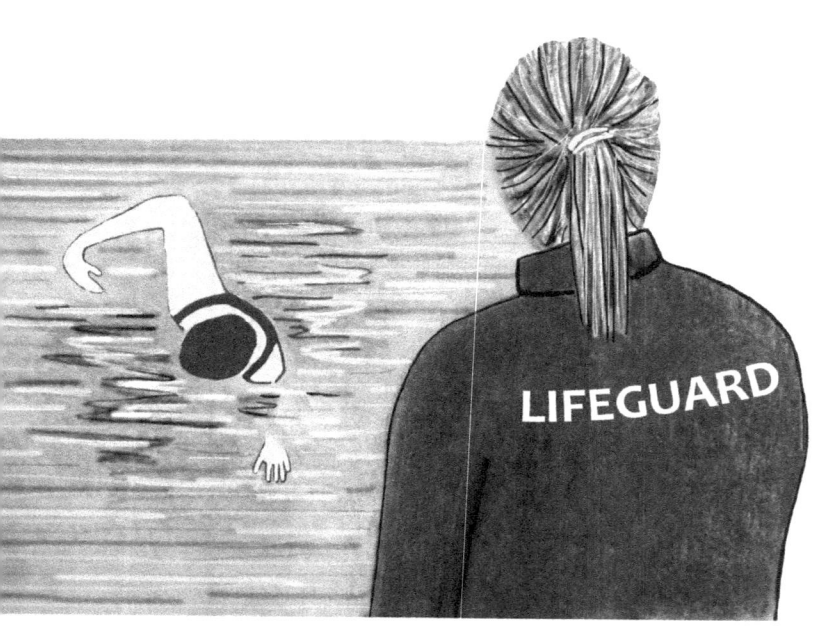

On some days, she would swiftly complete tasks.

Keep swimming, Mya!

I enthusiastically encouraged her to press on and keep doing her best. Occasionally, there were days when we simply pushed the textbooks aside, and I let her guide our conversation.

Sometimes, it's okay to tread water.

Mya spoke fondly of her grandmother, disclosed that she had never met her father, and resented her mother's lack of involvement. She pointed out that her mother didn't even know the names of her friends.

The most unsettling fact I uncovered through those casual conversations with Mya was that she had no vision for her future.

No hopes.

No dreams.

"Sometimes, life is overwhelming, and it may feel as though you are drowning. Mya, you are a strong girl. You can do hard things. When you feel the currents pulling you down, challenge yourself to keep searching for solutions.

Don't give up! Find the inner strength to try and save yourself.

And if it's too much, have the courage to call out for help."

I reminded Mya, "You are surrounded by teachers, family, and friends who want you to be successful. We're here for you. We believe in you."

I knew Mya had the potential to experience academic success, but only if her rescue team continued to balance high expectations with strong relationships and support.

On the final Thursday of the school year, everyone had gone home except for Mya, me, and the night custodians, a couple of whom stopped in to say hello and see why my door was still open. I sifted through a stack of papers and supervised Mya while she sat cross-legged on the floor, adding the finishing touches to her last assignment.

Tomorrow, the last day of school, students would gather for one final assembly.

Sunday	Monday	Tuesday	Wednesday	Thursday	Friday	Saturday
				1 ✓	2 ✓	3
4	5 ✓	6 ✓	7 ✓	8 ✓	9 ✓	10
11	12 ✓	13 ✓	14 ✓	15 ✓	16 ✓	17
18	19 ✓	20 ✓	21 ✓	22 ✓	23 ✓	24
25	26 ✓	27 ✓	28 ✓	29	30 Last day of school!	31

With her index finger hovering over the touchpad on her laptop, Mya turned to me, a pensive look on her face rather than the look of triumph I was expecting.

"Wish me luck," she whispered.

"Mya," I responded with a small smile. "Luck is a reflection of the choices we make and the actions we take. You've learned from your mistakes and worked hard on your essay.

There is nothing more you can do at this time. It'll be up to your teacher to determine your grade."

I pressed on, saying, "If you earn at least seventy percent on your essay, you will have passed *every* assignment, in *every* subject this year! More importantly, you've acquired knowledge and skills that will help you be successful in school and in life.

Mya, I've watched you learn to dream big this year, and you have taken steps toward making your dreams and goals become a reality. You can be proud of all that you have accomplished."

Mya shrugged and dipped her chin, but I could see a smile hiding behind her hair. Murmuring "3-2-1," she clicked Submit.

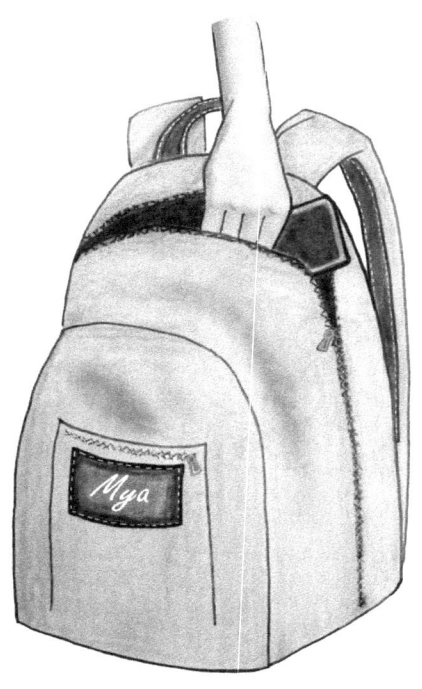

Digging into her purple backpack, Mya retrieved her phone and called her grandmother. "Grandma, I just finished my last assignment!" she proclaimed, excitement clear in her voice.

I heard love and joy in her grandmother's response, "I'm so happy for you, Mya. You must be so proud of yourself!"

With a beaming grin on her face, Mya hung up the phone and returned the laptop to her backpack. Walking shoulder to shoulder, we headed down the hall to her locker.

Exchanging her laptop for two novels, Mya flashed a smile as she stepped out the door. I watched her walk to her grandmother's car with joy in my heart, thinking about the progress this girl had made in the past several months.

Mya's middle school years were stormy, yet she persevered. Still, I found myself hesitant to let her move forward unsupervised.

Lifeguards know swimmers often appear to be fine, but at any moment, they can potentially slip quickly and quietly under the water. The same is true for struggling students.

What more can I do to help Mya stay afloat as she moves on to deeper waters?

As I walked into the gymnasium on the last day of school, hundreds of students sat on the bleachers, waiting for their final assembly to begin.

Mya had been on my mind since she turned in that final assignment. Even after watching her walk away the previous evening, her purple backpack bouncing a little with each excited stride, thoughts and questions about her future still ran through my mind.

The stark facts are intimidating: students who fail one core class in their freshman year are four times less likely to graduate from high school on time. Mathematics is the course Mya struggled with the most. I didn't want her to follow in her mother's footsteps and drop out, but I couldn't accompany her to her new school with her.

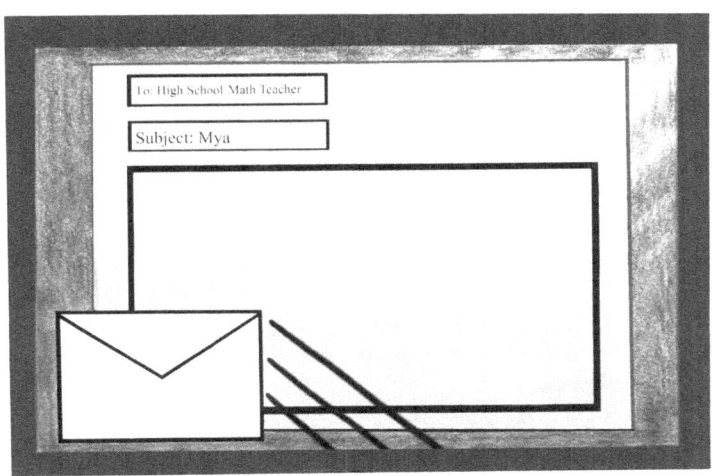

To: High School Math Teacher

Subject: Mya

With that in mind, earlier that day, I had reached out to the high school math teacher, who agreed to monitor Mya's grades and intervene early if she showed signs of struggling.

Likewise, I called the high school principal and counselor to explain Mya's family situation and ask them to keep a watchful eye on her from a distance.

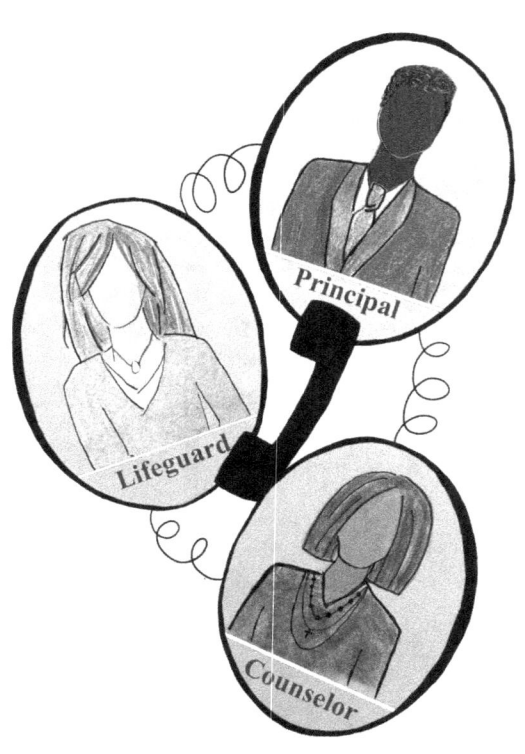

As I looked out over the assembly of eager students, I reminded myself of the learning lifeguards supporting Mya and made a mental note to occasionally invite her out to lunch next year—a simple way I could stay connected and show I was still there for her.

As if my thoughts had reached her ears, Mya's voice shouted out from the top row, "Ms. J, I'm going to miss you!" My eyes quickly scanned the sea of people, and I spotted her immediately … the one who had been on my watch for thirty weeks.

Mya sprinted down the bleachers, taking two steps at a time. Without saying a word, she wrapped her arms around me and squeezed me tight.

For eight months, she had clung to me for support, and now we both knew it was time to see if she could swim in deeper water.

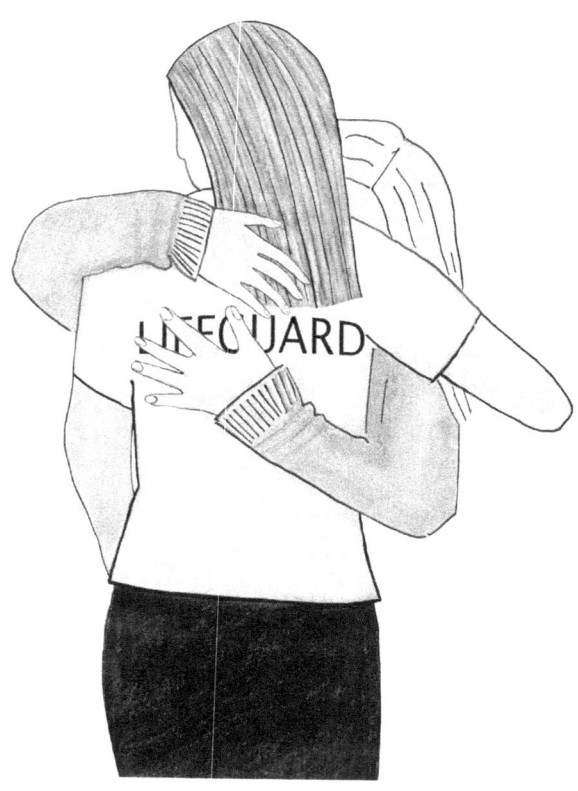

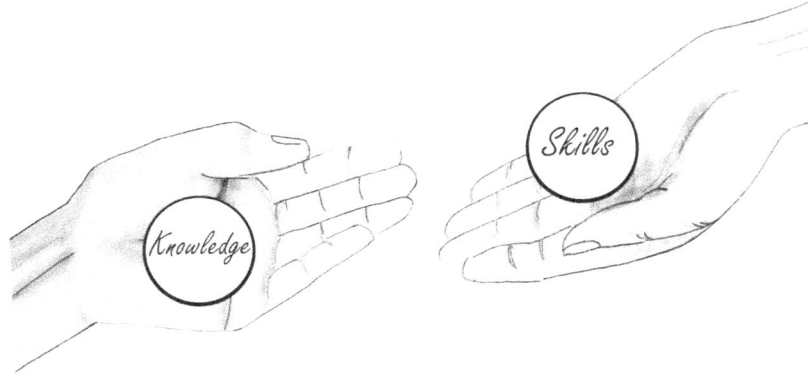

As Mya returned to her seat among her classmates who were also moving on to the next grade in a new school, a sudden realization hit me like a tidal wave crashing to the shore. Mya and I had **both** acquired new knowledge and skills from our time together.

Rather than surrender to her struggles, Mya was now engaged in her learning. She was discovering new self-rescue techniques. She practiced productive learning habits, and she stayed afloat by surrounding herself with positive people, asking for help, and accepting assistance.

Mya was determined to earn her high school diploma and dreamed of becoming an author one day.

Thinking back, I realized that students would rise and fall to the level of expectations we set for them, and the ebb and flow of our students' lives were constantly changing.

Rip currents often form, even on calm and sunny days. Those disturbances can temporarily zap a lifeguard's energy and strength, but the rewards that come from supporting students last a lifetime.

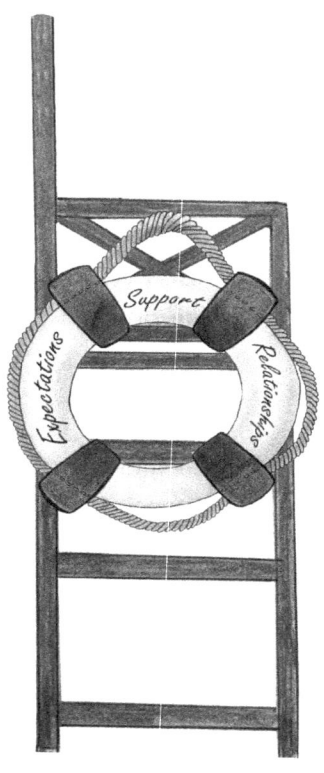

Every student needs a positive and caring adult to be on the lookout for turbulent tides.

Someone to help them navigate the challenges of school and life until they can confidently swim on their own.

A learning lifeguard.

My shift with Mya had come to an end.

I scanned the bleachers, searching for the next struggling student who needed assistance. The waters were deceptively calm.

My eyes detected a subtle ripple forming on
the horizon.

A sixth-grade boy slouched to the side on the top row. His hood was up and, for a brief moment, his guard was down. His eyes silently called out for help.

My next rescue shift had begun.

LIFEGUARD

"What's your favorite learning lifeguard memory?"

Clare, Grade 1
"We colored pictures."
Lifeguard: Bank Teller

Gabriella, Grade 2
"We ate lunch and watched puppy videos."
Lifeguard: Retiree

Armani, Grade 4
"He coached my soccer team!"
Lifeguard: Police Officer

Lila, Grade 4
"We played games she brought from her house."
Lifeguard: Bus Driver

Evie, Grade 6
"We wrote stories and poems."
Lifeguard: Library Assistant

Cal, Grade 6
"We ate together. Sometimes he brought lunch."
Lifeguard: District Administrator

MEMORIES

Mya,
I believe in you!
Ms. CJ

EJ, Grade 7
"We shot baskets in the gym."
Lifeguard: College Student

Mya, Grade 8
"She helped me with my homework."
Lifeguard: Instructional Coach

Theo, Grade 9
"He helped me finish my math assignments."
Lifeguard: Classroom Teacher

River, Grade 9
"We talked about the books we're reading."
Lifeguard: Case Manager

Tyrone, Grade 10
"He listened while I practiced my cello."
Lifeguard: Data Analyst

Cashton, Grade 12
"She helped me fill out applications."
Lifeguard: Sales Representative

FAQS

Can you explain the concepts behind learning lifeguards?

Swimming alone can be risky. However, the chance of drowning in the presence of a certified lifeguard is about one in eighteen million. Lifeguards give swimmers space within boundaries but watch closely and intervene if they suspect someone is in distress.

Similarly, each learning lifeguard seeks to support at least one underachieving student who is in danger of academically drowning.

Building a team of learning lifeguards doesn't have to be a complicated program or process. Simply:

- Determine what you want lifeguards to do.

- Identify the students who need extra support.

- Thoughtfully match each one with a trusted adult.

- Be a lifeguard!

The key is commitment. Each learning lifeguard should be willing to support their student for the full school year and, ideally, even longer.

Teachers who follow the learning lifeguard philosophy believe that all students can achieve high levels of learning if the adults around them show they care, collectively hold all learners to high expectations, and provide academic support to those who need it.

We recognize that the responsibility of helping our students reach their full potential cannot rest solely on the shoulders of a few; it requires a committed team. Research shows that just one trusted adult can have a profoundly positive influence on a child's life.

But how can we *really* make a difference?

Every interaction with a young person is an opportunity to influence the next generation.

Adults cannot fix everything, but we can consistently show up, listen, and guide. That's what learning lifeguards do, whether they're teachers, coaches, neighbors, college students, or community volunteers.

Learning lifeguards are caring adults who invest their time and hearts into helping students feel safe and supported. They build trust, provide a nurturing environment, and hold young people to high expectations.

Who can be a learning lifeguard?

In our school, every adult is a learning lifeguard.

Just imagine the life-changing impact we can make in our school and community if every staff member fostered a supportive relationship with at least one struggling student:

- Educational assistants help students finish assignments before school.

- Supervised high school students earn credits by tutoring other students during an open period in their school day.

- Teachers clarify misconceptions and reteach critical content after school.

- A custodian mentors a disruptive boy, more familiar with the principal's office than any classroom, by inviting him to tinker with tools and help with repairs around the school.

- The librarian offers her desk as a quiet place for a distracted student to complete her homework.

- The school secretary helps an unorganized student determine which assignment to tackle next.

- A basketball coach checks in daily to ensure the struggling sibling of a varsity athlete makes it to school.

So, anyone who has the commitment and the heart to help our students can be a learning lifeguard.

I don't work in a school. How can I help?

Community volunteers can become lifeguards, too! We take great care in thoughtfully matching our learning lifeguards to specific students, considering each adult's personal strengths and common interests with the students. This approach has expanded our lifeguard team and strengthened the safety net around our most vulnerable learners.

Sometimes, the most impactful learning lifeguards are community members who volunteer thirty minutes each week to mentor students in need of strong, supportive relationships. Many local business leaders generously offer their employees paid time off (beyond vacation days or personal time) to serve as volunteers in their community consistently. And often, universities and colleges partner with schools, encouraging their students to volunteer as mentors or lifeguards.

These lifeguards offer more than just their time:

- They create meaningful connections by providing students with the personalized support and attention they often crave but don't always receive.

- For younger students, that time might be spent reading together, playing catch or card games, sharing stories and riddles, or drawing and coloring.

- In middle school, lifeguards often help students finish their homework, study for tests, or get organized.

- Instead of scrolling on their phones during lunch, students may meet with their lifeguards, engaging in real conversations and learning how to connect face-to-face.

- Lifeguards might also coach a neighborhood sports team, offering students guidance both on and off the field.

- High school lifeguards might support students with their academic goals, explore college or career options, help with resumes or job applications, serve as thought partners, or simply offer a consistent and caring presence.

We need each other, and we need you.

DISCUSSION QUESTIONS

THESE DISCUSSION QUESTIONS are designed to deepen understanding and prompt readers of *The Lifeguard* to take action. You can answer the questions on your own; however, discussing the book with others is even better for building buy-in, strengthening connection, and promoting diversity of thought.

I encourage you to share your answers with another reader or form a discussion group. Here are some questions to start:

1. One empathetic and committed adult can change the trajectory of a student's life. Name a caring adult who empowered you when you were a student. What characteristics and strengths did that person possess? How did that person convey and support high expectations?

2. What do you feel are the essential attributes of an effective learning lifeguard? How can authentic relationships be fostered between students and learning lifeguards?

3. Multiple strategies were deployed to boost academic and relational support for Mya. Identify at least ten lifeguarding strategies within the story. Which tactic has the

potential to be most impactful for struggling students? Why?

4. Early identification of underperforming students puts them on the path to success. How do staff members proactively and systematically identify struggling students to ensure no one is missed? What information should you gather before determining resources and support?

5. We cannot expect to implement effective educational reform without support from *both* school personnel and the community. What are the benefits of collaboratively providing support to struggling students? How can we efficiently utilize caring adults to help all students reach their full potential?

6. As a community volunteer, what challenges would you expect to face when mentoring a student? How can you overcome these challenges?

7. A philosophy that doesn't get implemented is merely a suggestion. What training would your learning lifeguards need to support students effectively? How will learning lifeguards know if their rescue efforts are successful?

8. There is no trust if there are no boundaries. Building safe and trusting relationships with students requires strengthening

connections while maintaining personal and professional boundaries. How can learning lifeguards be compassionate and supportive without being intrusive?

9. Not every student is initially receptive to receiving support. How can we cultivate caring relationships and personalize our lifeguarding methods to ensure every child accepts the support they need?

10. Every interaction with a parent or guardian is an engagement opportunity. What steps would you have taken to rebuild the essential student-family-school relationship if Mya's grandmother and mother had not shown interest in academically supporting her?

11. Fostering a supportive learning environment requires service, persistence, and agility. How do learning lifeguards maintain stamina and prevent burnout while providing unconditional rescue support to students? What additional roadblocks might lifeguards encounter? How can staff monitor and support the ongoing implementation of the learning lifeguard philosophy?

YOUR CALL TO ACTION

EVERY STUDENT NEEDS a positive and caring adult to be on the lookout for turbulent tides … someone to help them navigate the challenges of school and life until they can confidently swim on their own.

Review your list of students.

Which struggling students have learning lifeguards? Which students do not? Who can step in and fulfill those roles?

What can YOU do?

Take that first step.

SHERRI'S FINAL WORDS

I believe adult learning can be fostered through literary fiction.

A GROWING BODY OF research has determined that reading fiction helps learners make sense of the world around them. Through fiction, readers "walk in the shoes of others," providing them with opportunities to view challenging situations from alternative perspectives. Researchers have found that readers of literary fiction, compared to readers of nonfiction, showed the most improvement on empathy tests. Furthermore, they have discovered that narrative fiction, used in an educational setting, has the potential to promote empathy, spark engagement, and enhance the professional development of school personnel.

Academic content can be effectively delivered through a simple story.

A recent study found that the average silent reading rate for adults reading fiction is 260 words per minute. Using this research as a guide, *The Lifeguard* can be read by a teacher during a single planning period within the school day.

Educators are often required to participate in collaborative learning communities where members are given the same book and meet with their colleagues to discuss the reading. This type of informal learning is designed to spark interest and build momentum for school initiatives.

However, many professional development books are heavy-laden with informational text that requires educators to carve out countless hours to plow through the content before meeting with their colleagues. Consequently, the strong readers and people-pleasers are usually the only ones who finish their reading assignments. The remaining group members often attempt to bluff their way through the professional discussions.

Yet reading the assigned book is only the first stage in the learning process. Participants need time to collectively assess their situation and develop implementation plans. Educators also need time to try out the new practices—to determine what works and what doesn't. Unfortunately, teachers often cite insufficient time to plan, prepare, and execute all the required tasks as the most common frustration.

If the goal of professional development is to effectively implement new ideas and strategies, then we must focus *less* on assigning teachers homework and *more* on the journey of learning, collaboration, and action.

My greatest hope is that everyone who begins reading *The Lifeguard* (by choice or at someone's request) finishes the book—not because they have to but because the simple story inspires them to reach for a rescue buoy and support a struggling student.

ABOUT THE AUTHOR

Sherri Nelson

Serving as a learning lifeguard while remaining employed full-time as an instructional leader allows Sherri to connect informally with students and reminds her why she chose to become an educator: She cares about kids and wants to impact their lives positively.

Sherri, a former middle school teacher and instructional coach, is currently the Director of Curriculum, Instruction, and Assessment for the Brandon Valley School District in South Dakota. A highly regarded educator for three decades, Sherri has worked as an instructional leader in two school districts on both ends of the student achievement continuum: a rural and low-income district (once identified by the state as requiring immediate improvement) and an affluent suburban district (recognized as being one of the best in the state). In both communities, she encountered students who demonstrated academic excellence with minimal assistance and those who needed extra support until they could independently navigate their academic journeys.

In her spare time, Sherri finds joy in connecting with educators nationwide and collaborating with them to develop plans for helping every student experience academic success.

She was recognized as South Dakota's Curriculum Leader of the Year in 2025 and honored as Huron Middle School's Teacher of the Year in 2011.

Sherri authored *Learning Lifeguards: Your 10-Step Guide to Building a Team that Motivates Struggling Students to Love Learning and Stay in School* and coauthored *The Brick House Study Guide*. Sherri has also contributed several articles and stories for educational publications and has presented the topic of academic lifeguarding at schools and educational conferences in twenty states.

Sherri and her husband are lifelong Minnesota Vikings football fans. They live in Brandon, South Dakota, and enjoy traveling and recreating their favorite restaurant dishes when they return home. Their two daughters teach in the neighboring school district, just eight miles down the road.

ABOUT THE ILLUSTRATOR

Abby Johnson-Youngquist

Abby Johnson-Youngquist is a Marketing Director and Artist based out of Sioux Falls, South Dakota. Her passion for photography, painting, and drawing developed at a young age. During her high school years, Abby enrolled in weekend classes at the Minneapolis Institute of Art, furthering her passion at the University of South Dakota, where she received her Bachelor of Fine Arts in Printmaking and a minor in Art History.

She went on to earn her Master of Business Administration from Capella University. During her college years, she enjoyed attending summer intensives at Frogman's Print Workshop.

Abby has taught screen printing techniques at several high schools and has been commissioned to create illustrations and paintings for teachers and their classrooms, most often in anatomical illustration.

Abby loves spending time with her husband and two children, whether hiking, gardening, traveling, biking, or relaxing by the water. She volunteers with youth mentoring programs and supports her community's foster care organization.

ACKNOWLEDGMENTS

Writing *THE LIFEGUARD* has been a tremendous gift to me. I feel deeply grateful for the opportunity to have spent three decades pursuing my calling, my passion, my purpose. Many of the insights in this book have emerged from relationships formed through the years with my colleagues, supervisors, mentors, students, friends, and family members. I will be eternally grateful to each and every one of them for teaching me how to be a better educator—and a better person.

Huron Middle School will always hold a special place in my heart. The lifeguarding method described in this book was primarily developed at HMS through research, experimentation, reflection, and revision. Depthless gratitude goes to Mike Taplett for giving me the opportunity to lead without a title. I will always cherish our problem-solving sessions held long after the buses pulled away. Thanks, too, to Laura Willemssen for sharing success stories when my confidence faltered. Knowing the tide was shifting fueled my desire to keep searching for solutions.

Special thanks to the HMS teachers and support staff for their willingness to try something new. Change is never easy, yet they pushed their discomfort aside and jumped in to support our struggling students. Thank you to my Exploratory teammates

(Michelle Johnson, Julie King, Teresa Smith, Doug Salter, Duane Boer, and Tim Buddenhagen) for their affirmation and candor. True friends always tell you like it is ... the good and the not-so-good.

The first community member to join our noble cause was Coach Swisher, a retired teacher. Steve's lifeguarding sessions after football practice provided academic support and reinforced the message that student comes before athlete. And every town should be so lucky to have someone whose connections and engagement have no boundaries. Rhonda Kludt relentlessly carried our lifeguarding message into the community, ensuring it reached far beyond the school walls.

We all need someone who helps us see things differently. I've come to appreciate the spirited debates I had with Terry Nebelsick. These conversations taught me that when your heart is in the right place, things work out in the end. I am also deeply grateful to my former students for providing insight into the academic and personal issues that young people grapple with. It's amazing what you can learn when you sit beside students while they work on their assignments.

Two Tennessee educators contributed more to this book and my career than anyone will ever know. The first is my dear friend Danny Hill, a successful author and founder of The Power of ICU. Danny introduced me to the lifeguarding concept and provided me with a platform to share my academic lifeguarding experiences with schools across the country. And then there is my trusted friend and mentor Jayson Nave.

Without question, this book would not exist without his moral support and guidance. Jayson taught me how to be a lifeguard. "Call if you need help," he said, and when I dialed his number week in and week out, Jayson picked up the phone. Every. Single. Time.

A chance encounter with a best-selling author led to the simplicity of the book you are holding in your hands. Damon West, coauthor of *The Coffee Bean*, was the first non-family reader of my manuscript, and I could not be more thankful for our newfound friendship. His praise gave me the confidence that I am, indeed, a writer.

Teachers sometimes impact the lives of their students without ever knowing it. On the last day of school when I was a junior high student, Mr. Anderson, my English teacher, showed our class the movie *To Sir, with Love*. Unbeknownst to him, that film sparked a desire within me to advocate for struggling students, which eventually contributed to the theme of this book. My high school English teacher, Mrs. Koffron, wasn't one to sugarcoat her words, but I must also acknowledge that her frank feedback made me a better writer.

My first written work appeared within the educational publications of the Association for Middle Level Education and the Association for Supervision and Curriculum Development. Their acceptance of my submitted articles made me realize that sharing my experiences could have a positive impact on students and teachers beyond the parameters of my school. I must also thank my educational author friends Ken

O'Connor and Tom Schimmer. Contributing content for their books inspired me to write my own.

Publishing a book isn't as simple as writing and printing a manuscript. I am grateful to the many people who helped me produce a quality product. Thanks to Kristina Johnson Mazourek for introducing me to her network of local creative contacts, including her husband, Michael Mazourek, who took my author photo, and my first editor, Maddie Mack. Maddie's suggestion to add dialogue brought my characters to life.

Additionally, I thank Mark Barnes, founder and president of Times 10 Publications, for being willing to try something new—using literary fiction to help adults better connect with students. My gratitude extends to his publishing team for their roles in bringing this book to life, especially Regina Bell, my project manager, whose understanding of how much this project means to me helped shape it into something truly special.

Thank you to my beta readers, Cheryl Puhl, Tony Thomas, Michelle Dolfuss, Lisa Emerson, Richard Hill, Karen Kennedy, Wendy Kullgren, Coen Martens, and Marie Palance for affirming that this book's message resonates with readers.

I am deeply indebted to Abby Johnson-Youngquist, the artist who created more than one hundred compelling illustrations for this project. It's only fitting that Abby and I collaborated on *The Lifeguard*, as our families have spent many glorious summers together at the lake.

I also thank my parents, Darrell and Julie, for raising strong girls and encouraging us to pursue our passions. My three sisters, Jaclyn, Melanie, and Michelle, were early readers of my manuscript. Their stamp of approval meant the world to me.

And finally, thank you to my husband, Bjorn, and our two daughters, Rachel and Jennifer—my learning lifeguards. They helped me navigate the high and low tides that come with writing a book. Without them holding me to high expectations and providing continuous support, I may never have gotten around to finishing my manuscript.

Everyone needs a learning lifeguard to help them stay afloat until they can confidently swim on their own.

WORKS REFERENCED

Brysbaert, Marc. "How Many Words Do We Read per Minute? A Review and Meta-Analysis of Reading Rate." *Journal of Memory and Language.* August 9, 2019.

Gillespie, Katie. "Ninth-Grade Failure Rates Reveal Much to State, Local Educators." *The Columbian.* May 14, 2018.

Hill, Danny, and Jason Nave. *Power of ICU.* NTLB Publishing. 2009.

Koppich, Julia. "Out-of-School Influences and Academic Success: Background, Parental Influence, Family Economic Status, Preparing for School, Physical and Mental Health." *stateuniversity.com.* 2019.

United States Lifeguard Association. "American Lifeguard Rescue and Drowning Statistics for Beaches." 2020.

ALSO BY SHERRI NELSON

Learning Lifeguards
Your 10-Step Guide to Building a Team that Motivates
Struggling Students to Love Learning and Stay in School
By Sherri Nelson

Many students grapple with academic riptides, desperately trying to stay afloat. As educators, do we turn away, or do we pool our resources and skills to prevent them from drowning? This empowering guide equips educators with actionable strategies for creating a school community where every student succeeds. Whether you're a teacher seeking solutions or a visionary principal, you can be an academic lifeline for your students.

BUY
LEARNING LIFEGUARDS

Available at:
10publications.com
Amazon.com
and bookstores near you

TIMES 10 PUBLICATIONS provides practical solutions that busy people can read today and use tomorrow. We bring you content from experienced researchers and practitioners, and we share it through books, podcasts, webinars, articles, events, and ongoing conversations on social media. Our books and materials help turn practice into action.

Stay in touch with us at 10Publications.com and follow our updates @10Publications.